STUDENT'S BOOK 2

SERIES EDITORS
Joan Kang Shin and
JoAnn (Jodi) Crandall

AUTHORS
Lesley Koustaff and
Susan Rivers

T0349580

1 **Listen.** What can you hear at the beginning? Match. TR: 0.1

I.

p
b
t
d
s
z
m
n
f
v
g
l

2.

3.

4.

5.

6.

7.

8.

9.

10.

II.

12.

2 Write the words. Then listen to check your answers.

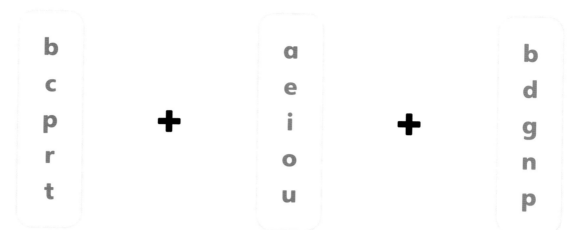

b		a		b
c		e		d
p	**+**	i	**+**	g
r		o		n
t		u		p

1.

_____

2.

_____

3.

_____

4.

_____

5.

_____

6.

_____

7.

_____

8.

_____

q.

_____

3 **Write the letters.** Have the words got the same sound? Listen and (circle) *Yes* or *No*. TR: 0.3

1.

d__ck   l__nch

Yes   No

2.

__awn   bab__

Yes   No

3.

__ake   jui__e

Yes   No

4.

e____   __oat

Yes   No

5.

fea__er   __ree

Yes   No

6.

b__s   s__gar

Yes   No

4 Follow the path to the words with the same sound.
Then listen to check your answers. TR: 0.4

th **th** **ch** **sh** **wh**

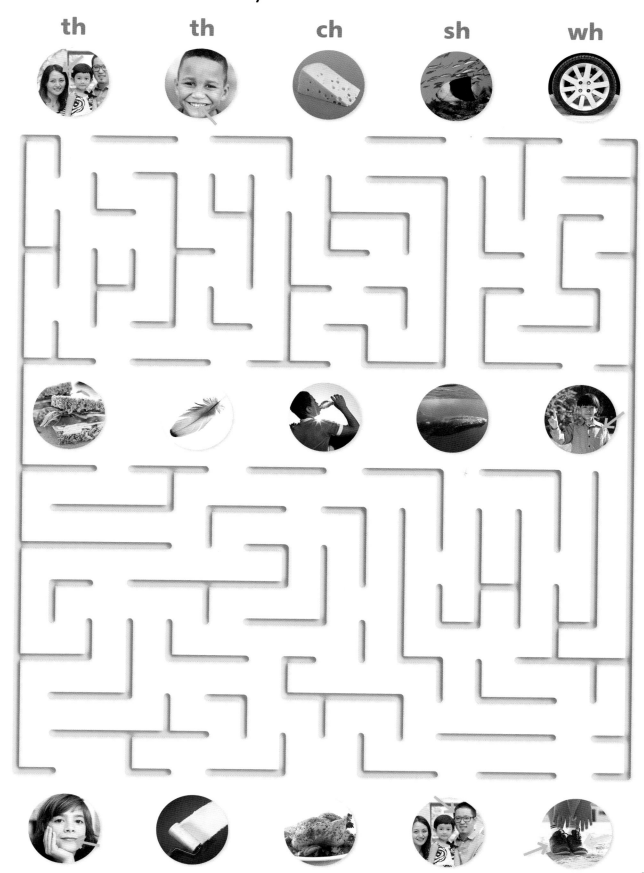

5 Is the sound at the beginning, in the middle or at the end? Listen and repeat. Tick. TR: 0.5

c

1.

2.

3.

4.

k

5.

6.

7.

8.

th

9.

10.

11.

12.

l

13.

14.

15.

16.

f

17.

18.

19.

20.

6 What sound can you hear? Listen and (circle.) TR: 0.6

1. k / x

2. k / x

3. k / x

4. k / x

5. a / e

6. a / e

7. a / e

8. a / e

9. i / o

10. i / o

11. i / o

12. i / o

13. ng / mb

14. ng / mb

15. ng / mb

16. ng / mb

17. ch / sh

18. ch / sh

19. ch / sh

20. ch / sh

7 Can you hear the word one or two times? Listen and
circle *1* or *2*. TR: 0.7

h

1. 1 2
2. 1 2
3. 1 2
4. 1 2

r

5. 1 2
6. 1 2
7. 1 2
8. 1 2

w

9. 1 2
10. 1 2
11. 1 2
12. 1 2

j

13. 1 2
14. 1 2
15. 1 2
16. 1 2

s

17. 1 2
18. 1 2
19. 1 2
20. 1 2

8 **Listen and write.** Then listen and chant. TR: 0.8

| c | k | mb | ng | u | x | wh | w | y |

J__mping in p__ddles, __ __ __.
P__shing and p__lling, __ __ __.
__ummy, __ummy __oghurt, __ __ __.
Ver__ mess__ day, __ __ __.

__ake and ice __ream, __ __ __.
A pretty pin__ __ite, __ __ __.
A ni__e red bi__ycle, __ __ __.
A T. re__ in a bo__, __ __ __.

A __orm in the __eeds, __ __ __.
___ere's the ___ite ___ale, ___ ___ ___?
Flyi___ birds si___i___, __ __ __.
Little la___s cli___ing, ___ ___ ___.

9 **Put the letters in order to make words.** Then listen and repeat. TR: 0.9

1.

hetfar

2.

sked

3.

kjetac

4.

gepa

5.

hnda

6.

cilnep

7.

plpea

8.

ngis

9.

orom

10.

lruooc

11.

llowey

12.

guars

13.

tnchkie

14.

llmas

15.

vrrie

16.

milafy

17.

vloe

18.

mlap

19.

phpya

20.

uckd

10 **Choose sixteen words from page 10.** Write them in the grid in pencil.

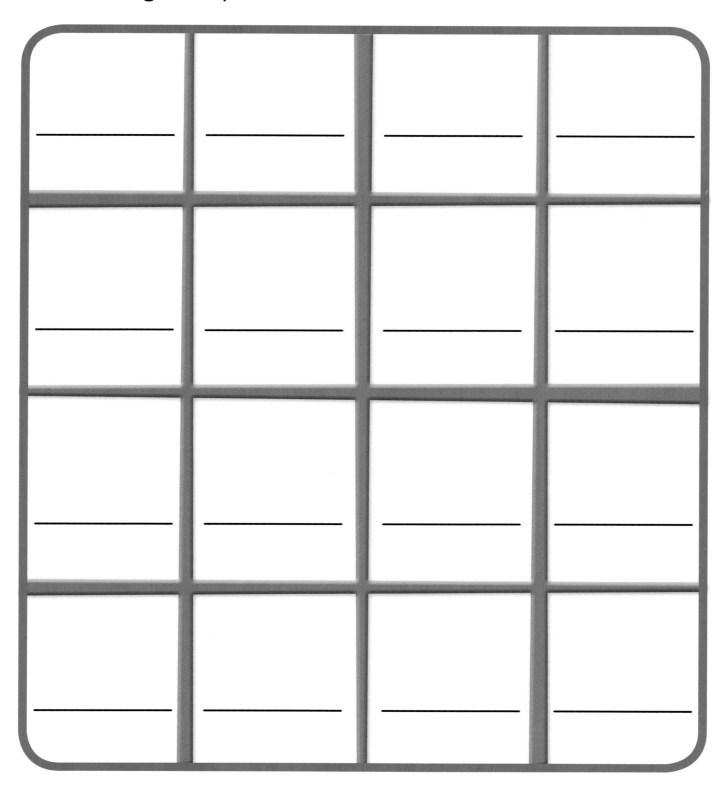

11 **Play *BINGO!*** Tick ✔ the words as you hear them.

1 **Listen.** Then listen and repeat. TR: 1.1 and 1.2

1.

b l ue

2.

b l ack

3.

b l ocks

4.

b l ouse

5.

b l anket

2 **Trace and say.**

3 **Can you hear bl?** Listen and circle *Yes* or *No*. TR: 1.3

I. Yes   No   2. Yes   No   3. Yes   No   4. Yes   No

4 **Can you hear the word with bl one or two times?**
Listen and circle *I* or *2*. TR: 1.4

I.    2.   3.   4.

I   2   I   2   I   2   I   2

5 **Listen.** Then listen and repeat. TR: 1.5 and 1.6

pl

1.
plane

2.
plant

3.

4.

5.

play   plus   plum

6 **Trace and say.**

7 **Can you hear pl?** Listen and (circle) Yes or No. TR: 1.7

1. Yes No   2. Yes No   3. Yes No   4. Yes No

8 **Can you hear bl or pl?** Listen and write. TR: 1.8

1.

2.

3.

4.

___ ___ate   ___ ___ink   ___ ___anet   ___ ___ender

9 **Listen.** Then listen and repeat. TR: 1.9 and 1.10

cl

1.

2.

class   clock

3.

4.

5.

cloud   clean   clothes

10 **Trace and say.**

11 **Can you hear cl?** Listen and (circle) Yes or No. TR: 1.11

1. Yes No   2. Yes No   3. Yes No   4. Yes No

12 **Can you hear the word with cl one or two times?**
Listen and (circle) 1 or 2. TR: 1.12

1.

2.

3.

4.

1 2   1 2   1 2   1 2

13 **Listen.** Then listen and repeat. TR: 1.13 and 1.14

gl

1.

gl ue

2.

gl ove

3.

4.

5.

gl ass   gl obe   gl ow

14 **Trace and say.**

15 **Can you hear gl?** Listen and (circle) Yes or No. TR: 1.15

1. Yes No   2. Yes No   3. Yes No   4. Yes No

16 **Can you hear cl or gl?** Listen and write. TR: 1.16

1.

2.

3.

4.

___ ___itter   ___ ___own   ___ ___asses   ___ ___aws

17 **Look and write the words.** Then listen and check. TR: 1.17

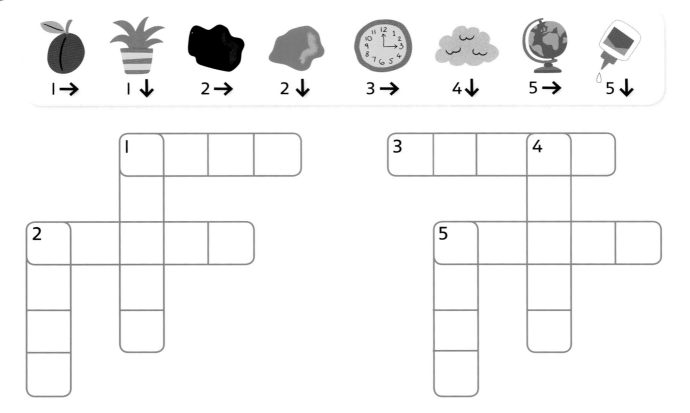

18 **Listen.** Then listen and chant. TR: 1.18

What are you doing?
Having some fun!
Who's having fun?
Everyone!

Playing with planets
and blue and black pens.
Making clowns with clay,
some glitter and glue.

What are you doing?
Having some fun!
Who's having fun?
Everyone!

19 **Listen.** Then listen and repeat. TR: 1.19 and 1.20

Art Class Fun

Gloria is gluing football players onto a playground.

Great!

Claudio is colouring black clouds in a blue sky. There are plum trees and plants, too.

Good!

Blake is making a clown with clay.

Lovely!

Clara is cutting paper for her plane.

Wow!

Wow!

Wow!

20 **Read the story.** Write *bl*, *pl*, *cl* or *gl*. Then go to page 78.

___ ___uing
¹ 2

___ ___oud
3 4

___ ___ue
5 6

___ ___ane
7 8

1 **Listen.** Then listen and repeat. TR: 2.1 and 2.2

pr

1.

2.

prince   prize

3.

4.

5.

proud   pretty   surprised

2 **Trace and say.**

3 **Can you hear pr or p?** Listen and (circle.) TR: 2.3

1. pr / p   2. pr / p   3. pr / p   4. pr / p

4 **Can you hear the word with pr one or two times?**
Listen and (circle) l or 2. TR: 2.4

1.

2.

3.

4.

l   2   l   2   l   2   l   2

5 **Listen.** Then listen and repeat. TR: 2.5 and 2.6

br

1.

2.

brown   brush

3.

4.

5.

bread   brother   umbrella

6 **Trace and say.**

7 **Can you hear br or b?** Listen and (circle.) TR: 2.7

1. br / b   2. br / b   3. br / b   4. br / b

8 **Can you hear pr or br?** Listen and write. TR: 2.8

1.

2.

3.

4.

___ ___incess   a___ ___icot   ze___ ___a   ___ ___acelet

9 **Listen.** Then listen and repeat. TR: 2.9 and 2.10

dr

1.

2.

dress   drum

3.

4.

5.

draw   dragon   children

10 **Trace and say.**

11 **Can you hear dr or d?** Listen and (circle.) TR: 2.11

1. dr / d   2. dr / d   3. dr / d   4. dr / d

12 **Can you hear the word with dr one or two times?**
Listen and (circle) / or 2. TR: 2.12

1.

2.

3.

4.

1 2   1 2   1 2   1 2

13 **Listen.** Then listen and repeat. TR: 2.13 and 2.14

cr

1.

crown

2.

cry

3.

crab

4.

crayon

5.

crumbs

14 **Trace and say.**

15 **Can you hear cr or c?** Listen and circle. TR: 2.15

1. cr / c   2. cr / c   3. cr / c   4. cr / c

16 **Can you hear pr, br, dr or cr?** Listen and write. TR: 2.16

1.

2.

3.

4.

___ ___ocodile   ___ ___inter   ___ ___oom   ___ ___ip

17 **Find and** (circle) **the words in the box.** Then listen and repeat to check your answers. TR: 2.17

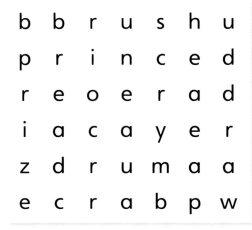

```
b  b  r  u  s  h  u
p  r  i  n  c  e  d
r  e  o  e  r  a  d
i  a  c  a  y  e  r
z  d  r  u  m  a  a
e  c  r  a  b  p  w
```

18 **Listen.** Then listen and chant. TR: 2.18

It's a fancy dress party.
Who can you see?
It's a fancy dress party.
Chant along with me.

Children dressed like dragons,
an acrobat with a crown.
The princess has got a present.
The zebra's umbrella is brown.

It's a fancy dress party.
Who can you see?
It's a fancy dress party.
Chant along with me.

The Dragon

Cristel is a princess. She's wearing a pretty dress. She's pretending to cry.

Brian is a prince. Look! The dragon is crawling near the prince and princess. Cristel protects Brian. She's very brave.

Drago is the dragon. The dragon jumps. Look! He breaks the princess's crown!

Oh, no! Look! The dragon head crashes to the floor! Drago is surprised.

20 **Read the story.** Write *pr*, *br*, *dr* or *cr*. Then go to page 78.

___ ___y   ___ ___ess   ___ ___ave   ___ ___ince
 l   2   3   4   5   6   7   8

1 **Listen.** Then listen and repeat. TR: 3.1 and 3.2

a_e

1.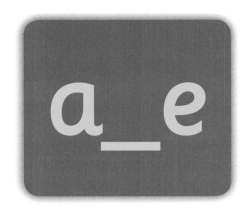

2.

b a s e b a l l   g a m e

3.    4.    5.

r o l l e r b l a d e   c a k e   s k a t e b o a r d

2 **Trace and say.**

3 **What words can you hear?** Listen and write the order 1 to 4. TR: 3.3

☐ cap   ☐ cape   ☐ tap   ☐ tape

4 **Can you hear a or a_e?** Listen and write. TR: 3.4

1.    2.    3.    4.

l__k__   wh__l__   f__n__   w__v__

5 **Listen.** Then listen and repeat. TR: 3.5 and 3.6

i_e

1.

2.

bike   hide

3.

4.

5.

rice   kite   dive

6 **Trace and say.**

7 **Can you hear i or i_e?** Listen and (circle.) TR: 3.7

1. i / i_e   2. i / i_e   3. i / i_e   4. i / i_e

8 **Can you hear a_e or i_e?** Listen and write. TR: 3.8

1.

2.

3.

4.

l__m__   c__v__   h__k__   f__c__

9 **Listen.** Then listen and repeat. TR: 3.9 and 3.10

1.

home

2.

rope

3.

phone

4.

nose

5.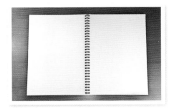

notebook

10 **Trace and say.**

11 **What words can you hear?** Listen and write the order
1 to 4. TR: 3.11

☐ hop   ☐ hope   ☐ rod   ☐ rode

12 **Can you hear a_e, i_e or o_e?** Listen and write. TR: 3.12

1.

2.

3.

4.

c___n___   w___v___   gl__b___   b___t___

13 **Listen.** Then listen and repeat. TR: 3.13 and 3.14

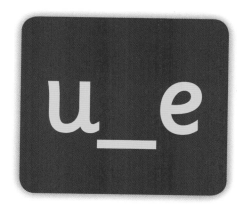

1.

flute

2.

June

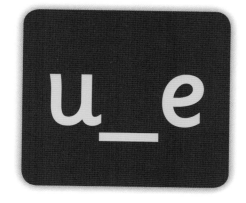

1.

cube

2.

mule

14 **Trace and say.**

15 **Can you hear u_e as in flute or u_e as in cube?** Listen. Write the numbers. TR: 3.15

u_e as in flute _____, _____   u_e as in cube _____, _____

16 **Can you hear a_e, i_e, o_e or u_e?** Listen and write. TR: 3.16

1.

2.

3.

4.

m___c___   J___n___   n___s___   g___t___

17 Follow the path to the letters that spell the word.
Then write the word.

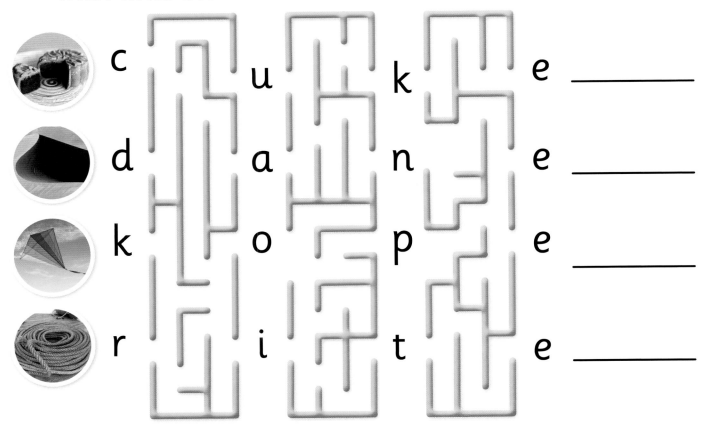

c   u   k   e _____

d   a   n   e _____

k   o   p   e _____

r   i   t   e _____

18 Listen. Then listen and chant. TR: 3.17

What do you do,
what do you do
when the sun shines
and the sky is blue?

We play baseball.
We ride our bikes.
We skip with ropes
and sing cute tunes.

What do you do,
what do you do
when the sun shines
and the sky is blue?

19 **Listen.** Then listen and repeat. TR: 3.18 and 3.19

A Day in the Sunshine

The sun shines in the sky. Cole and Kate ride their bikes to the lake.

Let's go, Kate!

Cole skateboards around the lake. Kate rollerblades.

Come on, Kate!

They hike up a huge dune and fly kites. Kate is tired!

Let's go home!

Kate, let's play baseball and skip with ropes. Oh, no! Wake up!

20 **Read the story.** Write a_e, i_e, o_e or u_e. Then go to page 78.

d__n__   l__k__   r__p__   r__d__
1   2   3   4   5   6   7   8

1 **Work in pairs.** Write the missing letters or put the letters in order to make words.

h___d_____

Start

Move forwards I space.

fetul

_____ack

_____ead

c___b___

hepno

bloge

nelap

_____ayon

r___p_____

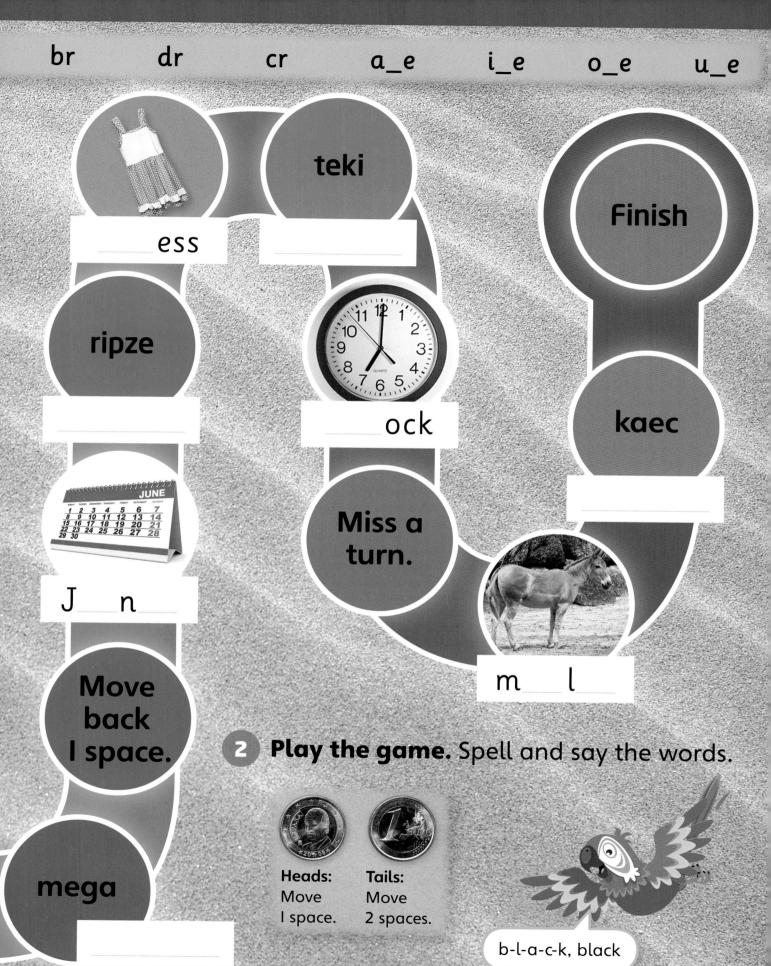

teki

_____ ess

Finish

ripze

_____ ock

kaec

JUNE

J__ n____

Miss a turn.

m__ l____

Move back I space.

2 **Play the game.** Spell and say the words.

mega

Heads: Move I space.

Tails: Move 2 spaces.

b-l-a-c-k, black

31

1 **Listen.** Then listen and repeat. TR: 4.1 and 4.2

ou

ow

1.

mouth

2.

house

1.

brown

2.

cow

2 **Trace and say.**

3 **Which words have got the ou/ow sound?** Listen and circle. TR: 4.3

ou
1.   2.

ow
1.   2.

4 **What word can you hear?** Listen and circle. TR: 4.4

1. now / no   2. spout / spot   3. town / tone   4. pound / pond

5 **Listen.** Then listen and repeat. TR: 4.5 and 4.6

1.

coin

2.

point

1.

toys

2.

boy

6 **Trace and say.**

7 **Can you hear the word with oi/oy one or two times?** Listen and (circle) I or 2. TR: 4.7

1. oy I 2   2. oi I 2   3. oi I 2   4. oy I 2

8 **Can you hear oi/oy or ou/ow?** Listen and (circle.) Write. TR: 4.8

1.

oy / ou

2.

oi / ow

3.

oy / ou

4.

oi / ow

___ ___ster   d___ ___n   sh___ ___t   b___ ___l

9 **Listen.** Then listen and repeat. TR: 4.9 and 4.10

cold   road   window

10 **Trace and say.**

11 **Can you hear the word with o/oa/ow one or two times?** Listen and circle 1 or 2. TR: 4.11

1.
2.
3.
4.

oa 1 2   ow 1 2   o 1 2   oa 1 2

12 **What words can you hear?** Listen and write the order 1 to 4. TR: 4.12

☐ go   ☐ goat   ☐ hello   ☐ bow

13 **Listen.** Then listen and repeat. TR: 4.13 and 4.14

1.

2.

bl_ue_   gl_ue_

1.

2.

fr_ui_t   j_ui_ce

14 **Trace and say.**

15 **Can you hear the word with ue/ui one or two times?**
Listen and (circle) *I* or *2*. TR: 4.15

1.

2.

3.

4.

ui   I   2   ui   I   2   ue   I   2   ue   I   2

16 **Can you hear ue/ui or ow/ou?** Listen and (circle.) Write. TR: 4.16

1.   ui / ow   2.   ue / ou   3.   ue / ou   4.   ui / ow

h___ ___   gl___ ___   m___ ___th   j___ ___ce

17 **Look and write the words.** Then listen and check. TR: 4.17

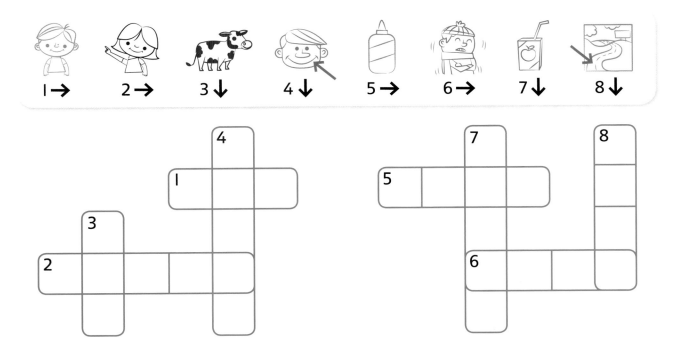

18 **Listen.** Then listen and chant. TR: 4.18

It's a snowy day.
Look at all the toys.
Come and chant with me.
Let's make some noise!

Where's the mouse?
It's in the house.
What's that noise?
It's Roy with his toys.
What's on the window?
Pretty white snow.
Sue loves juice.
Yes, that's true.

It's a snowy day.
Look at all the toys.
Come and chant with me.
Let's make some noise!

19 **Listen.** Then listen and repeat. TR: 4.19 and 4.20

Diego and Franco's New House

It's a cold, snowy day. Sofia puts on her blue snowsuit.

Hello, boys!

Hello! Can you come and see our new house?

They walk slowly in the snow.

There's just one room and one window.

That can't be true!

Sofia frowns.

Where do we go?

Down this road.

Diego points. Franco jumps for joy.

Wow! *That's* your new house?

Yes! Do you like it?

20 **Read the story.** Write *ow, oy, o* or *ue*. Then go to page 78.

tr___ ___   j_____   fr_____n   hell___
 1   2   3   4   5   6   7

1 **Listen.** Then listen and repeat. TR: 5.1 and 5.2

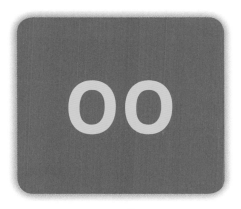

1.

2.

book   goodbye

3.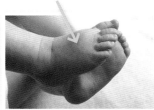

4.

5.

foot   wood   cook

2 **Trace and say.**

3 **Can you hear oo?** Listen and circle *Yes* or *No*. TR: 5.3

1. Yes No   2. Yes No   3. Yes No   4. Yes No

4 **Can you hear the word with oo one or two times?**
Listen and circle *1* or *2*. TR: 5.4

1.

2.

3.

4.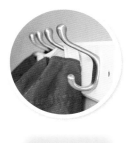

1 2   1 2   1 2   1 2

5 **Listen.** Then listen and repeat. TR: 5.5 and 5.6

oo

1.

food

2.

school

3.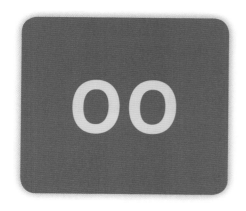

4.

5.

boots   pool   bedroom

6 **Trace and say.**

7 **Can you hear oo?** Listen and circle *Yes* or *No*. TR: 5.7

1. Yes No   2. Yes No   3. Yes No   4. Yes No

8 **Can you hear oo as in *good* or oo as in *food*?**
Listen and circle green or blue. TR: 5.8

1.    2.    3.    4.

9 **Listen.** Then listen and repeat. TR: 5.9 and 5.10

1.

eat

2.

teacher

1.

teeth

2.

sleep

10 **Trace and say.**

11 **Which words have got the ea/ee sound?** Listen and (circle.) TR: 5.11

ea

1. 2.

ee

1. 2.

12 **What words can you hear?** Listen and write the order
1 to *4*. TR: 5.12

red   read   met   meet

13 **Listen.** Then listen and repeat. TR: 5.13 and 5.14

1.

rain

2.

tail

1.

play

2.

today

14 **Trace and say.**

15 **Can you hear the word with ai/ay one or two times?**
Listen and circle 1 or 2. TR: 5.15

1. ay 1 2   2. ai 1 2   3. ay 1 2   4. ai 1 2

16 **Can you hear ai/ay or ee/ea?** Listen and circle. Write. TR: 5.16

1.    2.    3.    4.

ai / ea   ay / ee   ai / ea   ay / ee

b___ ___ns   cr___ ___on   tr___ ___n   s___ ___ds

41

17 **Find and circle the words in the box.** Then listen and repeat to check your answers. **TR: 5.17**

```
p o o l r f o o n
z c l t q s t j c
y b e d r o o m o
f v u s g d d r o
o s l e e p a a k
o b r w p b y i p
t e a c h e r n t
```

18 **Listen.** Then listen and chant. **TR: 5.18**

Saturday's our favourite day.
Chant with us, everyone!
Saturday's our favourite day.
It's always lots of fun!

I paint and play on Saturday.
I meet my team at noon.
I read a good book after dinner
when the moon shines in my room.

Saturday's our favourite day.
Chant with us, everyone!
Saturday's our favourite day.
It's always lots of fun!

19 **Listen.** Then listen and repeat. TR: 5.19 and 5.20

Lee's Day

Every day, Lee gets ready for school. He brushes his teeth in the bathroom.

He gets his books. Then he eats noodles. They're his favourite food.

After that, Lee and his dad walk down the street to school. Oh, no! Today, there's rain! Lee needs his hood.

Hi, Mr Dean.

Lee! Today is Saturday! Go home and play!

20 **Read the story.** Write *oo*, *ea*, *ee* or *ay*. Then go to page 79.

sch___ ___l   pl___ ___   str___ ___t   D___ ___n
   1   2   3   4   5   6   7   8

1 **Listen.** Then listen and repeat. TR: 6.1 and 6.2

walk   yawn   August

2 **Trace and say.**

3 **Can you hear al/aw/au?** Listen and circle Yes or No. TR: 6.3

1. Yes No   2. Yes No   3. Yes No   4. Yes No

4 **Can you hear the word with al/aw/au one or two times?** Listen and circle 1 or 2. TR: 6.4

1.    2.    3.    4.

aw 1 2   al 1 2   au 1 2   al 1 2

5 **Listen.** Then listen and repeat. TR: 6.5 and 6.6

1.

cry

2.

sky

1.

hungry

2.

thirsty

6 **Trace and say.**

7 **Which words have got the same y sound?** Listen and circle. TR: 6.7

y as in *cry*

1. 2.

y as in *hungry*

1.  2.

8 **Listen and repeat.** Write the words. TR: 6.8

1. _____ 2. _____ 3. _____ 4. _____

9 **Listen.** Then listen and repeat. TR: 6.9 and 6.10

1.

p ie

2.

fl ie s

1.

h igh

2.

l igh t

10 **Trace and say.**

11 **Which words have got the ie/igh sound?** Listen and circle. TR: 6.11

ie

1.

2.

igh

1.

2.

12 **Listen and repeat.** Circle three words that rhyme. TR: 6.12

pie   silly   sigh   happy   try

13 Listen. Then listen and repeat. TR: 6.13 and 6.14

ea

1.

br**ea**d

2.

h**ea**d

3.

4.

5.

sw**ea**ter   h**ea**vy   f**ea**ther

14 Trace and say.

15 Can you hear ea as in *bread* or ea as in *read*? Listen and (circle) green or blue. TR: 6.15

1.    2.    3.    4.

16 What word can you hear? Listen and (circle.) TR: 6.16

1. feather / father   2. bread / breed   3. sweat / sweet   4. head / hid

17 **Follow the path to the letters that spell the word.**
Then write the word.

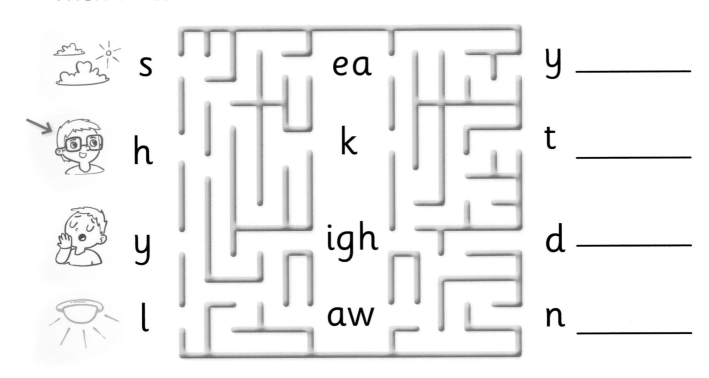

s   ea   y _____

h   k   t _____

y   igh   d _____

l   aw   n _____

18 **Listen.** Then listen and chant. TR: 6.17

Come on now, chant with me!
Don't be shy! Give it a try!

Oh, so happy!
I play football on the lawn.
Oh, so sunny!
I fly a kite in the sky.
Oh, so hungry!
I eat pie late at night.
Oh, so silly!
I draw bread on a head.

Come on now, chant with me!
Don't be shy! Give it a try!

19 **Listen.** Then listen and repeat. TR: 6.18 and 6.19

Paul's Silly Sister

Paul's baby sister starts to cry. He juggles small balls high in the air.

Why is my sister sad?

Is she cold?

Paul gets her a sweater. She isn't happy. It's too tight.

Is she tired?

The baby yawns. Paul turns off the light. She cries.

The baby is hungry! Paul gives her some strawberry pie. Look! It's on her head.

You're silly!

20 **Read the story.** Write *aw*, *al*, *ie* or *ea*. Then go to page 79.

b___ ___ls
 1   2

cr___ ___s
  3   4

h___ ___d
  5   6

y___ ___ns
  7   8

Review

1 Write the letters.

ou   ow   oy   oa   ui   oo   oo   ea
ee   ai   ay   aw   y   ie   igh   ea

sl___p

r___n

l__t

r___d

h___se

y___n

j___ce

t___cher

cr___

b___k

t___s

f___d

p___

br___n

br___d

pl___

2 **Write the words in the grid in pencil.** Use a different word order.

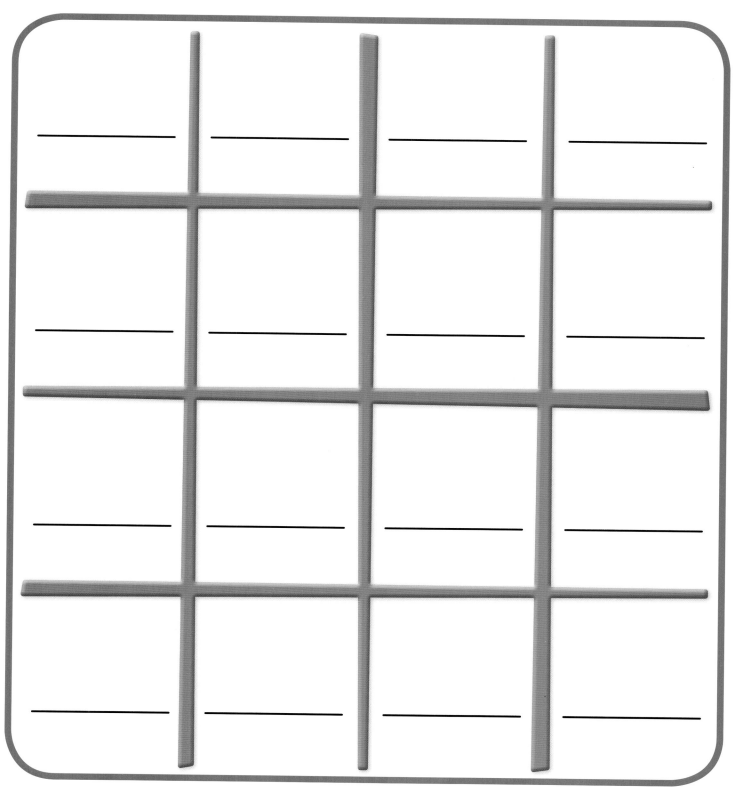

3 **Play *BINGO!*** Tick ✔ the words as you hear them.

1 **Listen.** Then listen and repeat. TR: 7.1 and 7.2

fl

1.

2.

fly   flute

3.

4.

5.

flag   flower snowflake

2 **Trace and say.**

3 **Can you hear fl?** Listen and (circle) Yes or No. TR: 7.3

1. Yes No   2. Yes No   3. Yes No   4. Yes No

4 **Can you hear the word with fl one or two times?**
Listen and (circle) 1 or 2. TR: 7.4

1.

2.

3.

4.

1 2   1 2   1 2   1 2

5 **Listen.** Then listen and repeat. TR: 7.5 and 7.6

fr

1.
2.

frog   friends

3.
4.
5.

frown   freckles   afraid

6 **Trace and say.**

7 **Can you hear fr?** Listen and (circle) *Yes* or *No*. TR: 7.7

1. Yes No   2. Yes No   3. Yes No   4. Yes No

8 **Can you hear fl or fr?** Listen and write. TR: 7.8

1.
2.
3.
4.

__ __ame   __ __oat   __ __uit   __ __y

9 **Listen.** Then listen and repeat. **TR: 7.9 and 7.10**

gr

1. 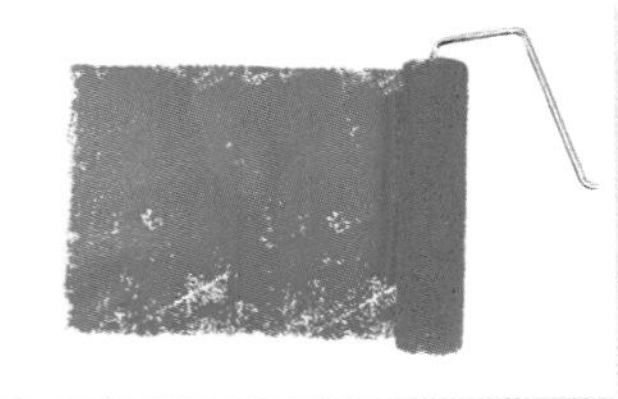

2. 

green grass

3. 

4. 

5. 

grandma angry playground

10 **Trace and say.**

11 **Can you hear gr?** Listen and circle *Yes* or *No*. **TR: 7.11**

1. Yes No
2. Yes No
3. Yes No
4. Yes No

12 **Can you hear gl or gr?** Listen and write. **TR: 7.12**

1. 

2. 

3. 

4. 

___ ___ove ___ ___in ___ ___apes ___ ___ow

13 Listen. Then listen and repeat. TR: 7.13 and 7.14

tr

1.
2.

trunk   tree

3.
4.
5.

train   triangle   controller

14 Trace and say.

15 Can you hear tr? Listen and (circle) *Yes* or *No*. TR: 7.15

1. Yes No   2. Yes No   3. Yes No   4. Yes No

16 Can you hear fl, fr, gr or tr? Listen and write. TR: 7.16

1.
2.
3.
4.

__ __uck   __ __eezer   __ __ey   __ __ip

17 **Look and write the words.** Then listen and check. TR: 7.17

1 →   2 →   3 ↓   4 ↓   5 →   6 →   7 ↓

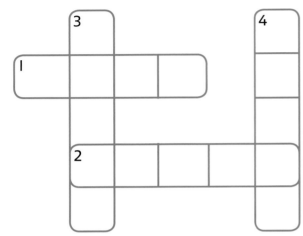
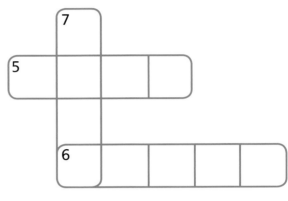

18 **Listen.** Then listen and chant. TR: 7.18

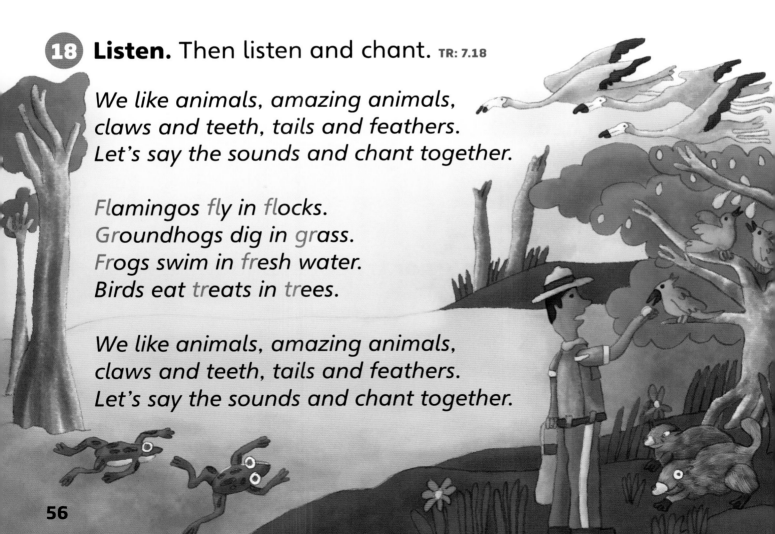

We like animals, amazing animals,
claws and teeth, tails and feathers.
Let's say the sounds and chant together.

Flamingos fly in flocks.
Groundhogs dig in grass.
Frogs swim in fresh water.
Birds eat treats in trees.

We like animals, amazing animals,
claws and teeth, tails and feathers.
Let's say the sounds and chant together.

56

Listen. Then listen and repeat. TR: 7.19 and 7.20

Why Is Frank Grumpy?

There are trees and flowers by a pond. Frank the frog lives there with his grandma.

Frank frowns. He's hungry and grumpy. His friends float away. 'Try to be nice,' says Flo the flamingo.

Frank sees a big fly. He grabs it and eats it. 'Oh, yummy! What a treat!' he says.

'I'm not hungry now,' Frank grins! 'That's great!' say his friends.

20 **Read the story.** Write *fl*, *fr*, *gr* or *tr*. Then go to page 79.

___ ___ o a t   ___ ___ e e s   ___ ___ o g   ___ ___ u m p y
 1   2   3   4   5   6   7   8

1 **Listen.** Then listen and repeat. TR: 8.1 and 8.2

I.

2.

s c **hool**   s c **ared**

I.

2.

s k **i**   **de** s k

2 **Trace and say.**

3 **Can you hear sc/sk or s?** Listen and ⟨circle.⟩ TR: 8.3

I.   sc / s   2.   sc / s   3.   sk / s   4.   sk / s

4 **Can you hear the word with sc/sk one or two times?** Listen and ⟨circle⟩ I or 2. TR: 8.4

I.

2.

3.

4.

sc I 2   sc I 2   sk I 2   sk I 2

5 **Listen.** Then listen and repeat. TR: 8.5 and 8.6

sl

1.
sl|ide

2.
sl|ow

3.

4.

5.

sl|oth   sl|ippers   a sl|eep

6 **Trace and say.**

7 **Can you hear sl or s?** Listen and circle. TR: 8.7

1. sl / s   2. sl / s   3. sl / s   4. sl / s

8 **Can you hear sk or sl?** Listen and write. TR: 8.8

1.

2.

3.

4.

__ __y   __ __edge   __ __ate   __ __eeve

59

9 **Listen.** Then listen and repeat. TR: 8.9 and 8.10

1.

sp**oon**

2.

sp ace

1.

star

2.

east

10 **Trace and say.**

11 **Can you hear sp as in *spoon* or st as in *star*?** Listen and (circle) green or blue. TR: 8.11

1. 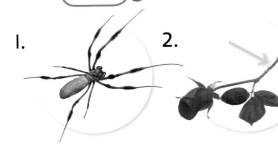 2. 3.  4.

12 **What word can you hear?** Listen and draw a line to make the word. TR: 8.12

1. sp	p	2. sp	ck	3. sp	ff	4. sp	ck
o		i		a		u	
st	t	st	n	st	n	st	n

13 **Listen.** Then listen and repeat. TR: 8.13 and 8.14

sw

1.

2.

swing   sweep

3.

4.

5.

swan   sweater   swim

14 **Trace and say.**

15 **Can you hear sw?** Listen and circle *Yes* or *No*. TR: 8.15

1. Yes No   2. Yes No   3. Yes No   4. Yes No

16 **Can you hear sc, sl, sp or sw?** Listen and write. TR: 8.16

1.

2.

3.

4.

__ __arf   __ __ug   __ __ipe   __ __inach

17 **Find and** (circle) **the words in the box.** Then listen and repeat to check your answers. TR: 8.17

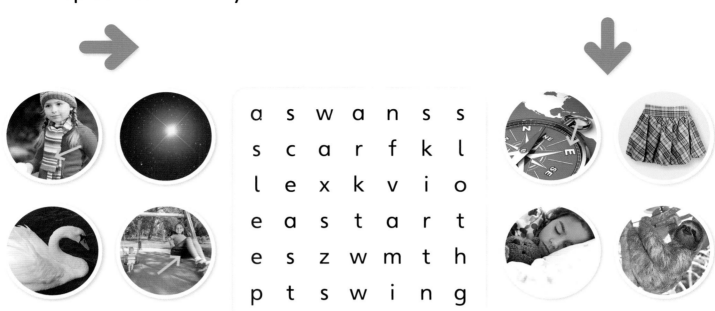

a	s	w	a	n	s	s
s	c	a	r	f	k	l
l	e	x	k	v	i	o
e	a	s	t	a	r	t
e	s	z	w	m	t	h
p	t	s	w	i	n	g

18 **Listen.** Then listen and chant. TR: 8.18

Work, work, wonderful work!
People work every day.
Work, work, wonderful work!
Chant and shout hooray.

The vet checks the sleepy sloths.
The actor wears a scary mask.
The chef makes spaghetti and steak.
The artist paints the swimming swans.

Work, work, wonderful work!
People work every day.
Work, work, wonderful work!
Chant and shout hooray.

19 **Listen.** Then listen and repeat. TR: 8.19 and 8.20

Slavik's Sculpture

The students are at school. They're at their desks in their art lesson.

What do you want to be?

Stefan sketches a sleepy sloth. He sketches a swan and a skunk, too.

A vet!

Slava makes a space station. It's very special.

An astronaut!

Slavik makes a sculpture. It looks like a film star.

A sculptor! Look! It's you, Mrs Slade!

20 **Read the story.** Write *sk, sl, st* or *sp*. Then go to page 79.

___ ___ecial   ___ ___oth   de___ ___s   ___ ___udents
 1   2   3   4   5   6   7   8

1 Listen. Then listen and repeat. TR: 9.1 and 9.2

sm

sn

1.

sm**all**

2.

sm**ile**

1.

sn**acks**

2.

sn**ow**

2 Trace and say.

3 Can you hear the word with sm or sn one or two times?
Listen and ⟨circle⟩ **I** or **2**. TR: 9.3

1. sm **I 2**   2. sn **I 2**   3. sm **I 2**   4. sn **I 2**

4 Can you hear sm or sn? Listen and write. TR: 9.4

1.

2.

3.

4.

__ __ake   __ __ail   __ __oke   __ __orkel

5 Listen. Then listen and repeat. TR: 9.5 and 9.6

cheese   mechanic   chef

6 Trace and say.

7 Listen and circle the words with ch as in *cheese*.
Then say all the words. TR: 9.7

1. ache   2. cheap   3. choose   4. machine

8 Can you hear ch as in *cheese* or ch as in *mechanic*?
Listen and circle green or blue. TR: 9.8

1.    2.    3.    4.

9 **Listen.** Then listen and repeat. TR: 9.9 and 9.10

1.

nuts

2.

grapes

1.

beans

2.

noodles

10 **Trace and say.**

11 **Listen and circle the words with s as in _beans_.** Then say all the words. TR: 9.11

1. snacks   2. buns   3. cats   4. monkeys

12 **Can you hear s as in _nuts_ or s as in _beans_?** Listen and circle green or blue. TR: 9.12

1.

2.

3.

4.

13 Listen. Then listen and repeat. TR: 9.13 and 9.14

es

1.

orang*es*

2.

pag*es*

3.

glass*es*

4.

bush*es*

5.

quizz*es*

14 Trace and say.

15 Listen and (circle) the words with es as in *oranges.*
Then say all the words. TR: 9.15

1. grapes
2. mangoes
3. boxes
4. watches

16 Can you hear s as in *nuts,* s as in *beans* or es as in *oranges?* Listen and (circle) green, blue or black. TR: 9.16

1.

2.

3.

4.

17 Follow the path to the letters that spell the word.
Then write the word.

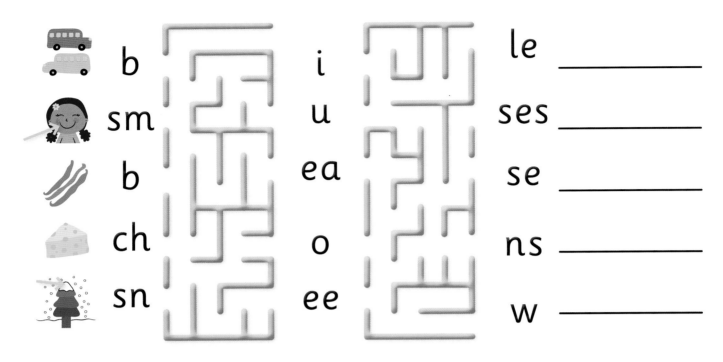

b	le _____
sm	ses _____
b	se _____
ch	ns _____
sn	w _____

i   u   ea   o   ee

18 Listen. Then listen and chant. TR: 9.17

Grapes, nuts, chips.
One, two, three.
We love snacks.
Chant with me!

Yummy snacks, big and small.
Mangoes, pears and carrots for us all.
The chef chops chocolate,
 peaches and cheese.
Give us oranges and sandwiches,
 please.

Grapes, nuts, chips.
One, two, three.
We love snacks.
Chant with me!

19 **Listen.** Then listen and repeat. TR: 9.18 and 9.19

Snap's Lunch

Meche is in the kitchen. She's making a snack. Nacho comes in.

You look like a chef!

Meche cuts peaches and bananas. She chops carrots and grapes.

Yummy!

She gets the fruit, the vegetables and some small flowers.

Yuck! My stomach!

Meche smiles. They're for her pet, Snap.

The sandwiches and chips are for us, Nacho!

20 **Read the story.** Write *sm*, *sn*, *ch* or *es*. Then go to page 80.

kit__ __en   peach__ __   __ __ack   __ __iles
  1   2   3   4   5   6   7   8

fl   fr   gr   tr   sc   sk

Start

crdsea

Move
forwards
I space.

ksrit

owns

lwrfeo

Move back I space.

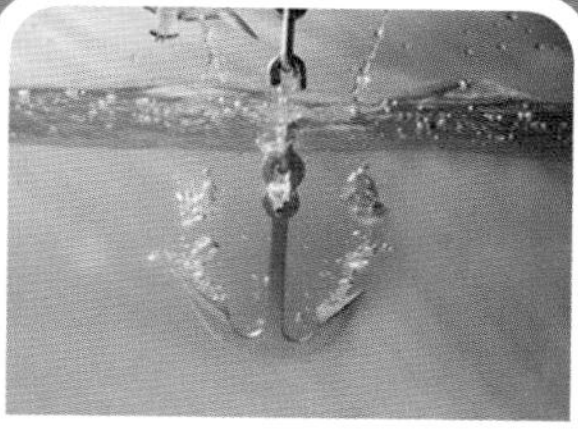

Finish

nahorc

wgsni

lslma

eidsl

1 **Work in pairs.** Write the words.
2 **Play the game.** Spell and say the words.

Heads: Move I space.

Tails: Move 2 spaces.

s-p-o-o-n, spoon

Picture Dictionary

1 bl pl cl gl

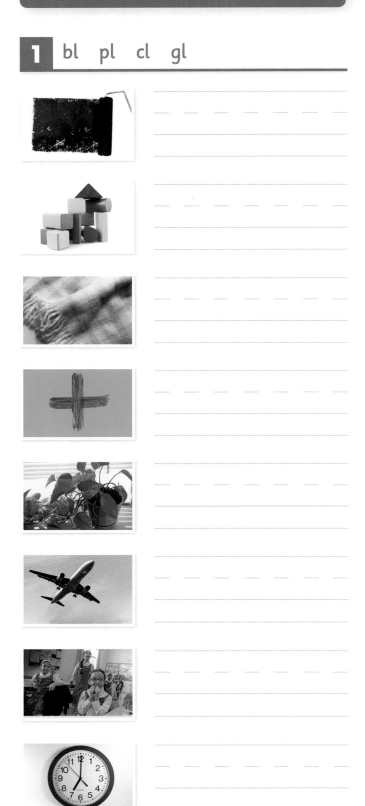

2 pr br dr cr

3 a_e i_e o_e u_e u_e

4 ou/ow oi/oy o/oa/ow ue/ui

6 al/aw/au y y ie/igh ea

7   fl   fr   gr   tr

_____

_____

_____

_____

_____

_____

_____

_____

_____

_____

_____

_____

8   sc/sk   sl   sp   st   sw

_____

_____

_____

_____

_____

Write the letters from Activity 20. Complete the sentence. Then finish the picture and colour.

Unit 1 Use with Activity 20 on page 17.

The ___ ___ ack ___ ___ ock in
     5 6   3 4

the ___ ___ a ssroom is big.
     3 4

Unit 2 Use with Activity 20 on page 23.

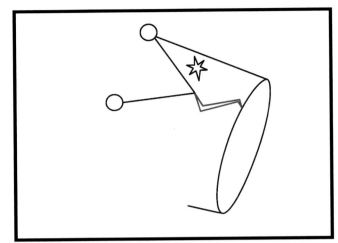

The ___ ___ agon ___ ___ eaks
     3 4   5 6

the ___ ___ etty ___ ___ own.
     7 8   1 2

Unit 3 Use with Activity 20 on page 29.

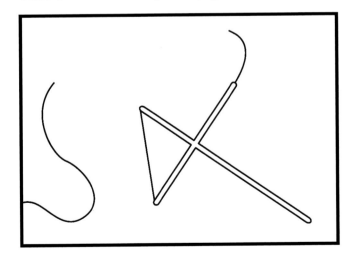

K___t___'s k___t___ is
  3   4   7   8

very c___t___.
       1 2

Unit 4 Use with Activity 20 on page 37.

Franc___'s t___ ___s are
       7   3 4

bl___ ___ and br___ ___n.
 1 2   5 6

Write the letters from Activity 20. Complete the sentence. Then finish the picture and colour.

Unit 5 Use with Activity 20 on page 43.

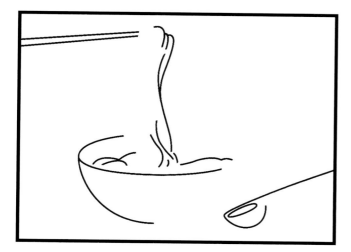

L__ __ __ __ts b__ __ f
  5 6   7 8   5 6

n__ __dles every d__ __.
 1 2   3 4

Unit 6 Use with Activity 20 on page 49.

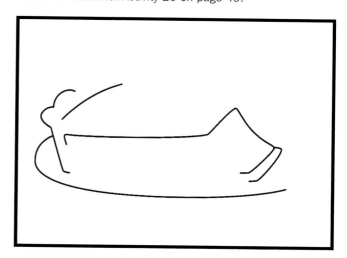

The str__ __berry p__ __
       7 8   3 4

is sm__ __l.
     1 2

Unit 7 Use with Activity 20 on page 57.

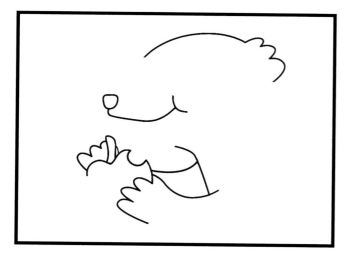

The __ __oundhog eats
      7 8

__ __uit from a __ __ee.
5 6   3 4

Unit 8 Use with Activity 20 on page 63.

__ __ava has got __ __ars
3 4   7 8

on her __ __ace __ __ation.
      1 2   7 8

Write the letters from Activity 20. Complete the sentence. Then finish the picture and colour.

Unit 9   Use with Activity 20 on page 69.

Me __ __ e has got two __ __ all dish __ __ for __ __ ap.
    1 2   7 8   3 4   5 6